Adjust Your Crown

The Little Ladies' Secret Handbook

Dionda Fugitt

Adjust Your Crown

Copyright © 2016 Dionda Fugitt
Cover Illustration by Dionda Fugitt & Waruwu
Studios

DiondaFugitt.com
Book design and production by Dionda Fugitt

ISBN-13:
978-1537021041

ISBN-10:
1537021044

*This book is dedicated to today's pretty little ladies. Yes darling, <u>YOU</u>! Hold your head high when you walk. Keep your chin up. Relax your shoulders. Bat your eyelashes a few times and strut your stuff... **umm** don't wiggle your butt. Just walk, smile and breathe. Only look down to fix your clothes and tie your shoes. When life gets tough,*
Adjust Your Crown *....and keep going.*

xoxo

This book is also dedicated to Sa'Niyah & Ja'Sai.

May you continue to be the amazing sparkly human beings you have always been. You two inspire me every day to be a free spirit. You bring out the best in me. You two have inspired me to follow my dream. Because of you, I am me and there is no other person I would rather be. You two are the definition of phenomenal.

insert secret handshake here

Table of Contents

Only **seven** Chapters?

Well, there are seven seas, seven continents, seven colors in the rainbow, and seven days of the week. WOW! Since you put it that way - this may just be a good book after all!

CLASS

"When someone is cruel and acts like a bully, we don't stoop to their level.
No, our motto is when they go low, we go high"
- Michelle Obama

In 2016, I have seen more little ladies learn the latest and most popular dance moves more than I have seen them have tea parties. Wait, do little ladies even have tea parties anymore? Do little ladies know how to cut their meat at the dinner table? Are they told to keep their elbows off the table? When you go to restaurants, do you see young ladies put their napkins in their lap and use their "inside voice"? Do not get me wrong, I am not expecting you to act as older women when you are still very young. B U T is anyone practicing proper etiquette anymore?

Let's bring <u>LADIES</u> back in style. When I say "<u>LADIES</u>", I am referring to the ladies in the real world that you see in your everyday life. I am referring to the ladies who cross their legs when they have a skirt on, the ladies who sit up straight with great posture and speak properly. I am referring to the ladies who use their napkin to dab their lips after a drink and use phrases like "excuse me", "thank you", "you are welcome" and "my pleasure". These are characteristics of a lady with class.

Regardless of status or demographics, I think *(and this is my opinion)* we need to get in to appreciating ourselves and putting ourselves on a pedestal. We, as young ladies, are pretty awesome individuals. We just need to remind ourselves every now and again. I want to reach out to every dazzling little lady and let her know that the knowledge she holds in her brain is way more important than anything she can ever buy, show off or put on. Now, let's have class.

(Signal the school bell)

Good Morning Students!

C.L.A.S.S. is now in session.

Today we will go over a few topics when it comes to being a young lady. Everyone, please get out your pretty colorful sheets of paper and pencils with the sparkles and glitter. Please write everything down and take clear notes. Ready? Let's get started.

Let's break **C.L.A.S.S.** down. What exactly is "class" you ask? Here goes.

Confidence – Your confidence shows in everything you do. Confidence is how you feel about yourself. Do you feel pretty? (You should, because you ARE!) Do you feel like you are the best swimmer? Do you feel like you are smart enough to pass the pop quiz in science class? Pretend your confidence is in an invisible crown. Wear your invisible crown everywhere you go. Wear your confidence crown to school, to sports practice, when you are in your room dancing and singing like you are a member of the Glitter Girls' rock band! Never forget to put it on. I try not to take my invisible confidence crown off. When my crown slips, I turn to my affirmations, which we will chat about that a little later.

Listen - You have two ears and one mouth. Listen to what is being said and let it sink in. Make sure you understand what is being said to you before you speak on it. You do not have to be the first person to scream out just any ol' answer to any ol' topic. There are times where I process what has been said to me twice, maybe even three times before I respond. It is definitely a great habit to form. Listen to advice from someone older than you whom you respect or look up to. Grandmothers and Grandfathers have some of the best advice on life's awesomeness. Sit and have a chat with your Grandparent(s), then go back and write down everything you learned from that chat. I am more than sure you could put it to good use one day!

Listen when no one is talking to you. When you are out for a walk, listen to the birds chirping. Listen to the cars riding by and the ice cream truck that is three streets away.

Have you ever sat in silence on a rainy day only to hear the rain hit your window or roof? It is one of the most relaxing parts of nature that I absolutely adore!

Speak – Speak on facts, things you know to be true. Stay far away from speaking on gossip and hateful words. It is just about the same as talking and seeing pollution come out of your mouth. EW! GROSS! Could you imagine how it would taste if every time you spoke negative, pollution and dark clouds came out of your mouth? Instead use your words to spread encouragement, peace and advancement. Speak positive vibes into the universe and the universe will definitely reward you in return. Speak on everything you believe in that spreads love + positivity. I promise everyone around will notice. OH - let's not forget this one, it is really important. When someone is speaking to you, look them in their eye. This will let them know they have your attention and you are fully focused. Did you notice how LISTEN is before SPEAK? hmmmm. Coincidence, or is it this way for a reason?

Selfish - That's right. I said it. Be selfish, but not egotistical. You know that one person who talks about themselves all the time, does not let you get one word in, constantly says "me, me, me, oh and then I.. oh and I ____ " -

THAT person is considered to be egotistical. When I say selfish, I mean in a positive way. When I say selfish, I mean investing in yourself first. You cannot be a great friend if you don't know who you are, where you are going in life nor what you want in life. You cannot have an open and honest conversation if you do not know yourself. There are small ways to invest in yourself daily so that it does not seem like a task the size of an elephant. Put yourself first by enhancing your vocabulary. Learn a new word every day. If you start in elementary, by the time you graduate from middle school you may have the vocabulary of a college student. Do you know how many doors you can open just from having a large vocabulary? A ton! Learning a new word daily does not have to take long. Open the dictionary while you are chomping down on your breakfast. The first age appropriate word your eyes land on, say it aloud. Read the definition aloud. Use that word at least twice within your day. There you have it. You are done. Do it again the next day, and so on...and so on.

My piece of selfishness is meditation. That's my *"me time"*. Whether I wake up before my alarm clocks goes off or lock myself in my room for twenty minutes after a long day, I have my *"me time"* every single day. I meditate to regain my calm spirit. Sometimes a busy day can leave us frazzled by the time we get home. You know that feeling after a long day at school that makes you want to go home and crawl under the blankets, right? Then you remember you still have homework and chores to do. This would be the time I would stop, drop and meditate to put myself back into a calm mindset. Once I am calm I think more clearly, make more conscious decisions, and get my tasks done with no problem.

Chapter Notes

What are some things you can do during your
"me time"?

What did you take away from this chapter?

Maintenance

"Be thankful for what you have; you'll end up having more. If you concentrate on what you don't have, you will never, ever have enough."
-Oprah Winfrey

Do you have an idol? Who is your favorite celebrity or well-known public figure? Why is she (or he) your favorite? Think really long and hard about your answer.

I believe we choose our idols and role models based on their specific qualities that we can relate to. Here's an example:

Who I admire: Oprah

Why: Because she was the underdog. She was doubted. No one believed she would succeed. She believed in her goals and she achieved them. Oprah is well known around the world but she does not brag about it. She remains classy, confident and humbled. If you notice, Oprah gives prizes away like we would share birthday cake. It shows her heart is pure and her intentions are good. She interviews people of success and great mindsets. When I say success, I am not only referring to those who are millionaires. I mean those who have loved, learned and have a powerful piece of knowledge to share. I do not know what she does in her spare time or private life, but in the public eye, she does not look down on anyone else. I believe Oprah would encourage everyone around her regardless of the life they currently have. I admire that. It makes me feel as if I hold the same power. WAIT - what am I talking about? I *do* hold the same power.

I believe we look up to certain people because we see a common interest or a piece of ourselves in that person. I admire Oprah because I am as powerful as she is. Maybe not as wealthy, but who says I cannot interview Deepak Chopra and Barack Obama, have my OWN television station and a magazine before I turn 50? Oprah reminds me that my power is within and once I find my super strength, I can (and will) make a difference in the world. Oprah reminds me that there are no limits. Think it. Believe it. Do it. I see myself in Oprah.

"Girls should never be afraid to be smart"
-Emma Watson

Regardless of who we choose to idolize, we all, no matter the age, have one common need - Maintenance. Maintaining yourself. Keeping yourself together. Properly caring for yourself. Regardless of your situation or where you stand in life, maintain yourself. Get plenty of exercise, choose what you eat wisely and drink plenty of water. Put (and keep) your clothes on properly. Keep your nails clean and eyes clear. If you wear your lovely hair strands straight, keep them brushed and tangle free. If you let your lovely locs free and blow with the wind, check on them every now and again to make sure they are in good condition. Make sure you are healthy - physically and mentally. Here are a few tips.

Physically - Get plenty of exercise. When I say exercise, I'm not talking about Army style training. Get off your electronics and go run outside. Have a race with your friends, hula hoop or play your favorite sport. Try as many new sports as you can. You are never too old or too cool to learn or try new things. I am still trying to hula hoop longer than five seconds. HA! Try to go for a walk, after you check in with your parent of course. Anything that will get your feet moving is good for your body. Be good to your body and it will be good to you.

Mentally - When you are not outside moving those feet, grab a book. Start reading a new book, *after* you finish this one of course. Choose an age appropriate book you would not normally read. Also, try learning an interested fact weekly, or even daily. Did you know, Blue Sharks are considered the wolves of the sea because they travel in packs? HA! Little known facts are so cool! Play a trivia game or make a goal to do long math problems in your head. First start small, then work your way to larger numbers.

What is 206 + 517?

Now, go bigger –

What's 1, 965, 70054 + 7,659,701?

No no no no! Don't go grab your calculator! Believe me when I say, you are smarter than you think. Take your time. Greatness takes time, patience and practice. Challenge yourself every week. I know you can do it. If you were not up for the challenge, you would not be reading this book! Imagine if you started doing math problems in your head for fun. Next thing you know, you had the chance to win one million dollars just for being a math genius! Hey, it could definitely happen. Anything is possible.

Chapter Notes

What new physical activities will you try?

Name two people you admire.
Why do you admire them?

Beyoutiful

"There is no greater
agony than bearing an
untold story inside you."
- Maya Angelou

Be **YOU** tiful. I have no idea who came up with that, but they are amazing! Why? Because - YOU are beautiful, when you are being yourself.

Who are you? YES - you have a name. But who is that person? What do you like to do for fun? What do you want to do with the rest of your life? You have an unlimited amount of years left on this earth and YOU can take the lead and design the life of your dreams. First, you must find out who you are. You can be a President, Astronaut or even the Doctor who cures all sicknesses. Starting today, get to know yourself. Find out who you are because you are someone's role model. You are the one who will turn someone's frown upside down. You are someone who will change the next person's outlook on life and possibly even save a life. You have the power to inspire and save the earth...or even Pluto, maybe Mars needs your help also, so let's get to it!

You have a story. Maybe you stood up to a bully or have become a spelling bee champion. You have a story. Whatever you have done thus far in life, it is extraordinary. If you are in 5th grade and have become friends with a preschooler then taught them geometry, that's a story be told! Do not be afraid to let your inner light shine. Everyone, including yourself, has a light inside of them that is waiting to shine. Do not hide your awesomeness. If you don't know how to start, ask your parents for help. It is time that we, as young ladies, get to know who we are and what our purpose is. We are all on earth to do something amazingly awesome. I am sure once you find your light, you will let it guide you.

With little to no guidance, it took me years to find my inner peace. It is just something that a lot of people do not talk about. While searching for my inner peace, I found a bit more. For instance, I have never been one to sit still long enough to focus on one long term goal. During my search for inner peace, I have learned that it is okay. It is actually exciting for some, like myself. I am a certified Medical Assistant, certified and well experienced Planner, Consultant and Coordinator with my own event logistics boutique (fancy schmancy for Event Planner's business), a half degree in Business Administration/Marketing major, as well as an author. I started writing poetry in middle school and have entered numerous contest. I have also written a series of books for toddlers! Now, at the time of writing this book, I have not yet published the series of books for toddlers, but they have been written. I have touched on all of my interest in life. I have glided every river my boat of life has floated and I have not fallen out. I have no regrets. WAIT! Let me clear the air. I am not telling you to skip out on college and be a hippie, unless you are great at it and that is your ultimate goal. I am simply saying this: be yourself and live your truth. If you truthfully love animals, love any and all animals of your choice. Be in love with animals and be great at loving animals. I am sure the animals will love you just as much. If you love to paint with your toes, do it and be great at it! Sale your toe paintings so you can make millions of dollars a month and paint for the rest of your life. Be who **YOU** are. Be-YOU-tiful! You deserve to be happy. You deserve to be <u>you</u> because, well honestly, <u>you</u> rock! Your parents designed you to be a perfect individual and that is what you are today. So be yourself and be great at being your amazing self.

"Today you are You, that is truer than true. There is no one alive who is Youer than You."
— *Dr. Seuss*

I believe in you! You have tons of people watching you who believe and admire you as well. Inspire them and let them know it is okay to be yourself; your gorgeous, beautiful self. Love who you are. Love your gross morning face because it is your gross morning booger face. Love your fingers and toes because believe it or not, your parents probably thought they were the most perfect baby fingers and toes they have ever seen.

You do not have any reason to believe that you are not a magnificent human being. We all have our bad days, believe me, I have had plenty. But what matters is, how many times you bounce back up from those bad days. Imagine yourself falling backward onto a trampoline and bouncing back up. That is what you will do daily, bounce back up!

There is a Japanese proverb that reads: "Fall down seven times, get up eight.ᶦ" This simply means, you are a survivor and a conqueror. You can fix any problem that comes your way. You can make it through any hard time, every trial and every negative situation. No matter how many times you may fall off the monkey bars, you will get back up and keep trying. You never give up. Keep in mind that every day is a new day and a fresh start. Never drag yesterday's rain storms into today's sunshine....ever! Leave it in the past. Focus on staying positive today and making every day after today wonderful. Have you ever noticed how you cannot plan for the past? There is a reason for it. It is done and over with. It is time to plan for the future, you can control that with no problem. Your past is not who you are destined to be.

You are destined to be bigger than your mistakes. If you dropped a bowl of spaghetti, it does not mean you will be known as the world's worst spaghetti dropper. You will be known as the girl who dropped spaghetti, cleaned it up on her own and moved on with her life. Do you want to know why? Because you – yes YOU – are awesomely amazing! Now go be great, with a dash of sparkly glitter on top!

Let's take all eyes off of you for a moment and chat about a well-known success story. Let's chat about Beyoncé. If you do not know who she is, here goes an introduction. Beyoncé is a singer, songwriter, actress and humanitarian, amongst a list of other great things. She started out with a girl group and later branched out into a solo career. Her career was once managed by her father. He assisted in bringing her career into what is it today. After years of singing what her fans liked. I believe one day she realized that she was molding into society's standards instead of being who she truly was. At some point, she decided to show another side of her that we assumed was there. Little did we know, this "new Beyoncé" was going to be epic! Beyoncé revealed to us that she was vulnerable, emotional, in love with life and all it has to offer and wanted to save the world. Most of all, she confirmed that she was human, just like her fans. To this very day, she is one artist who I enjoy wholeheartedly because I believe she knows who she truly is.

I know social media is huge now and it is okay to share bits and pieces. But once you let everyone in on your daily life and personal business, you allow them to have an opinion and an impact on your view of things. You begin to lose yourself and sometimes your happiness. Keep a large portion of your life private and never forget your values. Regardless of what everyone else is doing, your respect, your values, and your happiness are number one. This also comes with knowing who you are.

I believe that once you know yourself, and your value, you become one hundred percent happier. You know what you want to eat, you know where you want to go and you know whether you like blue colored shorts better than the green ones. Once you start to define who you are and what you really want it seems like the stars shine brighter; even your dessert taste better! Getting to know yourself might not be something that anyone can attain and perfect at the tender age of 10, possibly not even 14. It is something that is definitely worth working towards. You will learn so much on the journey.

Try keeping a diary, or journal if you prefer. Ask yourself random questions daily, sort of like you would ask a friend. Start with questions like: what is your favorite color? What are your hobbies? What is your favorite ice cream? What makes you the happiest? What makes you sad? Who are your best friends? Now do not laugh at me, but these are still questions I ask myself as an adult because I am constantly learning and liking new thing. Hey - what I like and dislike can change daily!

This is also fun to do with friends, and I mean your true friends. I am talking about the ones that you can cry to and not worry if they are going to make fun of you or go to school the next day and tell everyone you were crying. I mean the friends who are actually there for you. The ones who will hug you when you cry, tell you everything is going to be okay then check up on you the next day, and invite you over to laugh over a bowl of ice cream. Those are the friends who accept you and all your beauty.

Chapter Notes

What questions will you ask to learn more
about your beautiful self?

What are some of your special qualities?

Oh!
Hello
Confidence

"It takes nothing to join the crowd.
It takes everything to stand alone."
- Hans F. Hansen

Your confidence is how you feel about yourself, your powers and your overall level of awesomeness. Are you confident? Do you believe in your aspirations (goals)? When you fall down, do you pick yourself up or do you sit and cry while waiting for someone to give you a boost? Hold you head up beautiful! It is time for you to boost your self-assurance and confidence.

There was a time in my life where I cried about everything. My feelings were hurt by almost every conversation, comment and piece of feedback I received. I cried because my hair did not turn out just like the girl's hair in the magazine. I cried when none of my friends were available to hang out with me. I cried when the food I ordered did not taste as yummy as I imagined. I pretended to be a victim of everything. I'm not sure what I had for dinner the night before, but one day I woke up and told myself "enough is enough. I am exhausted from being sad and thinking so little of myself. I am naturally an amazing person." Literally, just like that, I made the decision to pick myself up and change my outlook on life. I told (and still tell) myself daily, I AM A FABULOUSLY AMAZING INDIVIDUAL! There are days I prefer to think I am a butterfly, but who does not want to be a butterfly, right? Sometimes, I put on lip gloss with the glitter just so I feel a little more fabulous. The best way to build your self-esteem, is (drum roll please)...STOP comparing yourself. You, my darling darling beauty, are amazing, truly amazing. Like, your bones are super shiny and have glitter on them, kind of amazing! I am not just saying anything in this book to be "nice". I am being genuine. You cannot compare yourself to anyone else. There is no one other human being that has the same miraculous molecules as you do. Awesomeness is in your DNA my friend.

 Before you do this, pinky promise that you will be one hundred percent truthful and honest when you write this stuff down. Once it is on paper, you cannot take it back! So, here goes: Make a list with two columns.

Who I Am | Who I Will Be

On the left, make a list of who you are. Make sure fabulous is at the top of that list, please and thank you! Then fill in the rest. Are you a piano player, science lover or naturalist? Write it! Are you someone who is a big sister, great at math or a great car washer? Write It. Make your list as long as you want, because you are pretty awesome and have a lot of awesome qualities! Once you have completed that side, think about who you <u>will</u> be. This can be the person you will be tomorrow, next school year or even in 10 years. It does not matter. What matters is that you put it on paper. Now, read it aloud. Reading your list aloud puts positivity in the air and sets the standards for your goals.

Keep this list. Put it under your pillow or tape it on your mirror. Just make sure you read and update it often. Remind yourself how amazing you are and how many great qualities you have going for yourself. This is where great self-esteem will begin. Re-write this list as often as you would like and keep building yourself up. Although it is enjoyable and sometimes helpful, you do not need anyone else to tell you how astonishing you are. As long as you have this list, you have already told yourself.

Keep in mind all of the moments in life where you did something you were proud of. When was the last time you got an outstanding grade on a test or project and felt proud of it? Did you tell your friends, parents and family members? Oh, and how about that time you were there for a friend who needed you? I am sure your friend will not forget it and neither should you!

Those who have a positive role in your life, keep them close by. Pay attention to the friends who cheer for you when you are doing great and are always around when you need them most. Friends are always helpful when it comes to keeping your self-esteem boat sailing! Be there for your friends as they are for you.

Another quality to building confidence, is honesty. I believe when you are honest, you have nothing to hide. When you have nothing to hide, you feel freer. Imagine a bird trying to fly with rocks on its back. It would be pretty tough for that bird to fly. Imagine how high that same bird can soar without rocks. Pretty high right? Those rocks weighing the bird down are similar to the "untruths" some people carry around with them. When you lie, or tell things that are not true, you have to lie to cover that lie. Lying only leads to more lies. The number one person you must be one hundred percent honest with, is yourself. Now, if you are telling a small fib to your BFF because you know about their surprise birthday party, I'll let that one slide.

You do not have to be a model or the center of attention to be worthy. Do not base your life off of "likes" or how many friends you have online or in person. You, as you stand today, are powerful just as you are. Now now, don't go lifting boulders because I reminded you of your powers! Work smarter, not necessarily harder. Instead of trying to lift the boulder on your own, call over a few friends and lift the boulder together. We are girls! We rock! Did you see how I put boulder and rock together? HA! After you lift that boulder, place it back on the ground and fix your crown!

Chapter Notes

Who are you friends that make you happy?

What are you most proud of?

GOALS

"In the end, it's not the years in your life that count. It's the life in your years."

-Abraham Lincoln

GET OUT AND LIVE SOME

When I see the word GOALS, this is what comes to mind. Unless your goal is to sit around and do nothing, every goal you set will require you to live a little. A "goal" is the end result of your actions once you set out to do something. When I say "live some", it doesn't necessarily mean you have to pack your bags immediately and travel to another continent, although I would advise you do so once in your life. Set your goals high. Everything is within your reach. It all depends on what you are willing to work for. From my experience, I have learned that you have to step outside of your comfort zone to reach your goals, or else they would not be goals. They would be in the "been there, done that" category.

One of my most recent goals was to get all of these thoughts, everything in this book, out of my head and put them on paper. I felt like there was no need in keeping my thoughts to myself and hoping to meet a little lady who could read my mind and would benefit from the positivity juiciness I have stored in my brain. So, I became best friends with a pen and paper….and my laptop, mobile notepad, calendar and talk to text app on my phone. I had to put my thoughts on paper, immediately. I would record myself talking aloud, just so I could get it out of my head. The edits would come later, but the thoughts were random and non-stop. Since you are reading this book, I am sure you can guess that my goal has been achieved! Woohhooo! Whether it be mental, physical or emotional, your goals will make you stronger.

Mental goals can be anything from "I want to add twenty new words to my vocabulary over the summer" to "I want to be able to finish the new math game in under four minutes". Anything that will add to your comprehension skills and help you to think logically would be a mental goal. Training your brain to be more swift, tough and full of knowledge is a mental goal. We should all have at least one mental goal per week. I can pinky promise that there are major benefits from setting mental goals and achieving them.

Physical goals will make our bodies stronger. Example: I want to do one hundred sit-ups every day. Your physical goal can entail you being active in Physical Education class, running one mile, doing twenty-five jumping jacks and so many other activities. Physical goals are extremely important because our bodies depend on us. What you put into physical goals is what you will get out of it. Give it all you've got and keep telling yourself to keep going. Please talk to your parents and/or a supervising adult before, during and after physical activities. Be sure to let someone know if you are not feeling well before, during or after a physical activity. I would hate for one of my dazzling and darling ladies to be injured in any type of way. Currently, my goal is to get in shape. To reach my goal, I have become more active and have signed up for an exercise class, which I absolutely adore! When you exercise, your body releases chemicals called endorphins[2]. Endorphins run around your body and opens the doors of positivity.

#PositiveVibesOnly

Emotional goals are goals we make based off of feelings. "I want to stop crying over things I cannot change". This, my lovely butterflies, was a goal of mine for a very long time. Emotional goals can be a large list of things, but they are all based off feelings.

Here are some ideas:

Goal	How To Reach Your Goal
I want to be grateful	Say "thank you" often
I do not want to worry	Take deep breaths and try to focus on everything that is positive.
I want to handle situations that would normally make me cry.	Gather your thoughts and try to figure out why you are crying. Take a deep breathe (*(I do this a lot as you can see)* and put on your crown. Ask for help with the situation. Think of yourself as stepping on a cookie crumb. Pretend the problem is the cookie crumb. Do not be afraid of it, just smash it! Build up your courage and tackle the problem.
I want to be happy, all the time.	Write down what makes you happy daily. Slow down and enjoy life. Stop and smell the roses every once in a while. Most importantly, take deep slow breathes!

These are all emotional goals that are attainable. I have been there and I have gotten through just fine. You can do it too. You got this! You are more than capable of achieving these goals, and so many others as long as you put your mind to it.

 Get a notepad and keep your goals aligned, just like the stars. Make your goals shine bright so that you have no problem seeing them. No goal is unrealistic. If you can think of it, you can get it done. It's all on how you plan to accomplish it. Goals may be more enjoyable when you bring a friend along. So grab your bestie and write down some goals!!

Chapter Notes

What are your goals for this year?

Who is your best friend? When will you and your best friend write down your goals?

Meditation + Affirmations

"In a world full of models,
let's be mermaids."
-Dionda Fugitt

According to Wikipedia, meditation is a practice where an individual trains the mind or induces a mode of consciousness, either to realize some benefit or for the mind to simply acknowledge its content without becoming identified with that content, or as an end in itself [3]. What in Jupiter could that possibly mean? Well, let me break this down for you. When I first started looking into meditation, that definition did absolutely nothing for me. It was gibberish and written for people who lived on Jupiter. Simply put, mediation is "*me time*". During this *me time*, it is best if you focus on your breathing. Inhaling love and positivity then exhaling hate and negativity. The other benefits come along on their own. Breathe in and breathe out. Actually, stop what you're doing and put this book down. Well, maybe you should reading these steps, then put the book down.

Here goes:

Step 1:	Find a completely silent space. My room is my favorite place.
Step 2:	Sit in a comfy spot.
Step 3:	Crisscross applesauce. You know, with your legs crossed Indian style.
Step 4:	Correct your posture by sitting up straight. No slouching. Make sure you are sitting as tall as possible. Keep your crown on your head. Do not tilt your body and allow it to fall.

Step 5:   Feel free to put your hands on
            your knees or in your lap. You
            can also touch your middle
            finger and thumb together,
            making an "O" shape and rest
            your wrists on your knees.

Step 6:   Inhale - Slowly take a deep
            breathe in through your nose.
            Hold it in for 2 seconds

Step 7   Exhale - Push all of that bad air
            out through your mouth.

Congratulations! You just did the Sukhasana pose and your first meditation exercise! Do this over and over, as long as time allows or until you feel relaxed. There is no time restriction on meditation. Do it as you please and do it however makes you comfortable.

I came across meditation as I was searching for a way to live a life that was more enjoyable and where stress did not take over my life. You know that feeling you get of butterflies fluttering in your stomach right before a big test? How about the feeling you get when you are frustrated while doing homework? Yikes! I really do not like that feeling. When you learn to properly meditate and the power meditation has, you worry less. In my opinion, it helps to meditate before you study before a test. Those butterflies fly right out of the window and into the sky. Sometimes I meditate in the morning before I start my day. This gives me a calm and relaxed feeling and keeps me from feeling rushed and antsy early in the morning.

There is quite a list of benefits when it comes to meditation, some I had not thought of. Like, body awareness, self-awareness, regulation of emotion and regulation of attention[4]. Thinking more clearly is definitely a major plus. Who does not want to be on top of everything at all times? I know I do! Imagine your parents quizzing you with math problems before your big test. Now, imagine you calculating and shouting out the answers with no second guessing and brushing your lovely locs all at the same time. You would know how to solve those problems flawlessly without butterflies, sweating or panicking because your mind is simply at ease. You are a smart young lady. You have the power to relax and be great at the same time. Meditating will help you relax and embrace your powers. Try it once every night before bedtime. Note how I said before bedtime right? Don't wait until your parents say "bedtime darling" and begin to meditate. Try it five to ten minutes before bed so your mind and body are relaxed. Meditation is tough, so just focus on breathing first. It took me months to get it to where I feel comfortable meditating, so don't rush it.

"Don't ask yourself what the world needs. Ask yourself what makes you come alive and then go do that. Because what the world needs is people who have come alive."
— *Howard Thurman*

Affirmations.

I absolutely love affirmations. When you speak something into existence, it's an affirmation. It's speaking positivity and your goals into being truths. Notice how the word "firm" is in af<u>firm</u>ation? It is there because your affirmations are firm, strong and true. Here's an example:

Goal: I want to be the best soccer player in my entire school.

Affirmation: I have the knowledge, strength and talent to be the best soccer player in my entire school.

Affirmations can be anything you want them to be, as long as it is all positive. Affirmations are motivation and a way to influence yourself to be great. Affirmations helped me a ton while I was switching over to live a more positive life. Positive thoughts and statements said aloud bring on positive energy. Positive energy brings on positive results. I like to get ready in the morning and before walking out the door, I like to look in the mirror and repeat my affirmations. Sometimes while I'm doing my hair, I would speak them aloud while looking in the mirror. Some of my favorite affirmations are:

"Be strong. Be True. Be you"

"I am confident and courageous.

"I am strong, intelligent

and fearfully fearlesss"

These are just a few of the affirmations I enjoy repeating. Feel free to start with these and make a list of your own that help you have a brighter and better day. If you feed your mind love and positivity, you will have a life full of it.

You know how we remember the words of songs? Repetition. We hear the songs on the radio two to three times every day. Next thing you know, we know all of the words to the songs, the rhythm of the song and even the background beats. Do you know how powerful you can be if you say the affirmations aloud, or even to yourself, two to three times a day? You would be unstoppable because you are telling your mind that you are unstoppable and ready to take on anything that comes your way!

Chapter Notes

What are two affirmations you will say daily?

How long do you think you can meditate?

Fearfully Fearlesss

"What would you attempt to do if you knew you could not fail?"
(unknown)

Do you see how there is an additional "s" on fearlesss? This was done purposely. I want you to stretch out the word "fearlesss" because it has far more meaning than you can ever imagine.

Living fearfully fearlesss began as just a journey for me. I wanted to change a few things in my life but was far too afraid to just wake up and do it without preparing for it. I could not see myself just dropping everything I knew, all the knowledge I accumulated and just start a new life. Nope. Na-uh! No thanks! That was way too scary for me. Change filled me with fear. Doing what I have always done was comfortable for me. A change meant "new"; new people, new duties, new insight, new clothes, new friends, new food….and the list goes on and on. Now that I think of it, all of that actually sounds exciting! What I have learned in the fearfully fearlesss process is this: When you are on any journey, you must find the glitter lining. Glitter lining? Sounds cool, but what is it? Let us sprinkle a little glitter on a few situations.

> ## *"If you only do what you can do, you'll never be better than what you are"*
> -Master Shefu, Kung Fu Panda 3

The Glitter Lining

When I began yoga, I went straight to Bikram yoga. Oh geesh. It was soo hot, like over one hundred degrees kind of hot, and I had not learned any of the yoga moves before going to class. It seemed like everyone in my entire class were professionals and I was the only beginner. I felt as if I could not catch my breath for the first fifteen minutes. My hair was messy. I felt like my toes were two hundred feet away from my body. I had sweat dripping in my eyes and totally forgot my towel to clean my face at home. Gross! Yet, once I stopped the negative thoughts that were running a marathon in my head, I began to inhale and exhale at ease. *Wait - this is not bad at all. This is actually relaxing. Inhale. Hold it in. Exhale. Namaste. Woah! Wait a minute. I can do this. I am good at this. This is really cool!* I was super excited and was anxious for the next class. I sprinkled a little glitter on that hot and sticky class and found the glitter lining.

Some may say silver lining. But hey, we are young ladies who are adjusting our crowns. We are going to call it the *glitter lining*. Fancy huh?!

The glitter lining is seeing the positive side of every situation. If you are practicing or training to run a marathon, your feet may hurt at the end of the day. However, you are becoming stronger and healthier every minute you are in training. If you win a gold medal, like the sparkly one Simone Biles and Simone Manuel⁵ now own, that would be the icing on the cake! Sprinkle a little glitter on that training session and voila - you have a glitter lining. If you have to read for one hour after school as a part of your homework, it may be a little boring. However, your brain is getting exercise and you may be building

your vocabulary without realizing it!
Sprinkle a little glitter on that reading session
and guess what? You have a glitter lining.
Focus on the positives and that one hour will
not be so bad!

The goal is to connect every moment
of your beautiful life with positivity.
Everything you do in life is way better when
you are surrounded by positive vibes. Find
the glitter lining in people as well. Your older
sister may not be fun all of the time, but she
sure does give good advice. You have found
a glitter lining.

When you live a *fearfully fearlesss*
life, you become a strong young lady with

every second of the day. During this journey, you are gaining confidence as well.

> ## *"Say it. Believe It. Do it. Tackle Fear."*
> *-Dionda Fugitt*

Now, it is time to open the door, kick fear in the behind and boot the crazy thing all the way across the street. From this moment on you are no longer afraid. Here are a few fun facts to remember while you begin this journey:

Fearfully Fearlesss Fun Fact #1

When you shake hands - have a firm grip. This lets people know you are a lady but you mean business. You are the boss of your own destiny, it's time to take charge! You do not have to squeeze the other person's hand and make it red. Yikes! A firm grip will do just fine. We do not want to reveal our super powers just yet!

Fearfully Fearlesss Fun Fact #2

Don't be afraid to use your voice darling. When you speak you hold power. Let us not get ahead of ourselves and think we have presidential power immediately. Your power comes from knowledge. If you know what $50 + 50$ equals, speak up and say the answer. "$50 + 50 = 100$." Speak loud and clearly. There is power in your voice as a young lady. Use it. Never be afraid to speak up. As long as what you are saying is one hundred percent truth, use your voice.

Fearfully Fearlesss Fun Fact #3

Power comes from within, it is your mindset. If you believe, you can achieve. That goes for everything you do in life.

Fearfully Fearlesss Fun Fact #4

Learn to be compassionate to your fellow lady. It is an amazing feeling when we pick each other up and are there for each other. Only a young lady who lives fearfully fearlesss has the courage to make friends with a new young lady. Be the leader. Make a new friend. You two may have more in common than you may ever know. She may be the only girl in school who enjoys chocolate ice cream topped with gummy worms, raisins, walnuts, cereal and cherries just like you! You and your fearfully fearlesss friends can do amazing things together.

"Be Bold –
you were born that way!"
-Dionda Fugitt

Did you know that most successful people can write a script about their life? They know what they want, how they will get it and what they will do with it. Do you know what your future holds? You will not get what you want if you do not know what you want. What do you want to do today? Think about it and give a genuine answer. Do not answer what you think you are supposed to want. But give yourself an answer for what you really want. I want to make an A++ on my test; I want to make a new friend; I do not want to be friends with ___ because they don't want what is best for me; I want to save fifteen dollars by Saturday so I can go buy a new shirt.

Know what you want and go for it. There are a ton of millionaires in the world today. As you are reading this book, most of them are not sitting on their bottoms watching cartoons. They are gaining better skills in their sport so they can become the best at what they do. They are reading, just like you are right now. They are learning and actively gaining more knowledge to be better than they were yesterday. So take a moment and pat yourself on the back for doing the same thing a millionaire - someone with a master plan for their life - is doing at this very moment. You are already on your way to a wealthy life!

How are they doing these things? **FEARLESSLY**! They are waking up every morning with a plan to lead a fearfully fearlesss life and to go after their goals.

Have you ever felt like ....blaaahhh? You know that "I do not feel like doing anything" feeling? Have you ever had a day where you woke up and did not want to move your stinky bottom out of the bed? If you have not, I would personally like to meet you because I have those "I want to keep my stinky bottom in bed" days often. BUT I find the glitter lining in those moments. I use those moments to tell myself "move it or lose it lady". I either have to get up and enjoy the day or lay in bed while a great day of life moves on by. Each day, remind yourself to live in the moment. If it is raining outside, go jump in a puddle. If it is sunny after your homework is done, ask your parents if you can go to the playground or hang out with friends. Enjoy life's simplest moments!

Be A L I V E

Aspire. Love. Inspire. Value. Encourage

Each day that goes by, aspire. Try something new. It does not have to be anything dramatic. It can be a new food or even a new word that you have learned the definition to. If you believe in yourself other people will believe in you and will follow your lead of believing in themselves. You never know how far you can go if you never try.

Each day that goes by, love. Whether you hug your parents a little tighter or you say "I love you" more than once, show a bit more love every day. I secretly believe that love can change the world, possibly save it from any and everything. Love can turn your day from negative to positive in a short time span. Love a little more today than you did the yesterday. Show love to your fellow lady friends.

Each day that goes by, inspire. Be your own idol. You can inspire everyone around you just by being your true self. Your natural beauty may inspire someone to embrace their natural beauty. Your smile may inspire someone to smile and be more positive. Inspire your fellow lady friends. Your positive energy and attitude may inspire someone to never give up and to see the glitter lining in their everyday life.

Each day that goes by, value it. Value yourself. Show yourself how important you are. This can be done in a few minutes with your affirmations and/or meditation. After that is done value someone else. This can be something as simple as telling your brother or sister "I value you. You are important to me".

"Dance in glitter, but protect your gold".
-Dionda Fugitt

This quote is a saying that I recite a lot. In so many words, it states that it is okay to sparkle and shine, but do not forget your value. In today's world, diamonds and all things shiny are put on a high pedestal. Values are things that are important to you. Examples of values can be your education, your quality time with your family or even your favorite teddy bear from your Grandparents. What are your values? Write them down. Live by them and protect them.

"Boys compete. Ladies empower."
-Dionda Fugitt

Each day that goes by, encourage. Encourage yourself with affirmations, written or said aloud. I do this a lot and it makes me feel phenomenal. Encourage a friend or family member to do something they may be afraid to do, only if it makes them better. Be the opposite of envy. When you feel like you are starting to think negative of or about someone, catch yourself and change it immediately. Switch to a compliment. Go to the girl you almost said something negative about, and compliment her on her shoes, her hair, or her outfit. Encourage your friends and family to be great. Encourage them by telling them how awesome they are. Teach them what the glitter lining is and how to find.

"DO NOT

GROW

UP…. EVER."

*"Mature. But don't grow up
Keep your imagination
flowing. It is what will keep
you happy and your positive
energy flowing!"*
-Dionda Fugitt

[1]"Japanese Proverbs." Wikipedia. Wikimedia Foundation, n.d. Web. 09 Sept. 2016. | [2]"Exercise and Depression: Endorphins, Reducing Stress, and More." WebMD. WebMD, n.d. Web. 09 Sept. 2016. | [3]"Meditation." Wikipedia. Wikimedia Foundation, n.d. Web. 09 Sept. 2016. | [4] Chan, Amanda L. "Mindfulness Meditation Benefits: 20 Reasons Why It's Good For Your Mental And Physical Health." The Huffington Post, 08 Apr. 2013. Web. | [5] 2016 Olympics www.olympic.org

Book Notes

_____

_____

_____

_____

_____

_____

_____

_____

Book Notes

_____

_____

_____

_____

_____

_____

_____

_____

Book Notes

_____

_____

_____

_____

_____

_____

_____

_____

Book Notes

_____

_____

_____

_____

_____

_____

_____

Book Notes

CPSIA information can be obtained
at www.ICGtesting.com
Printed in the USA
LVHW04s1437260918
591442LV00009B/472/P